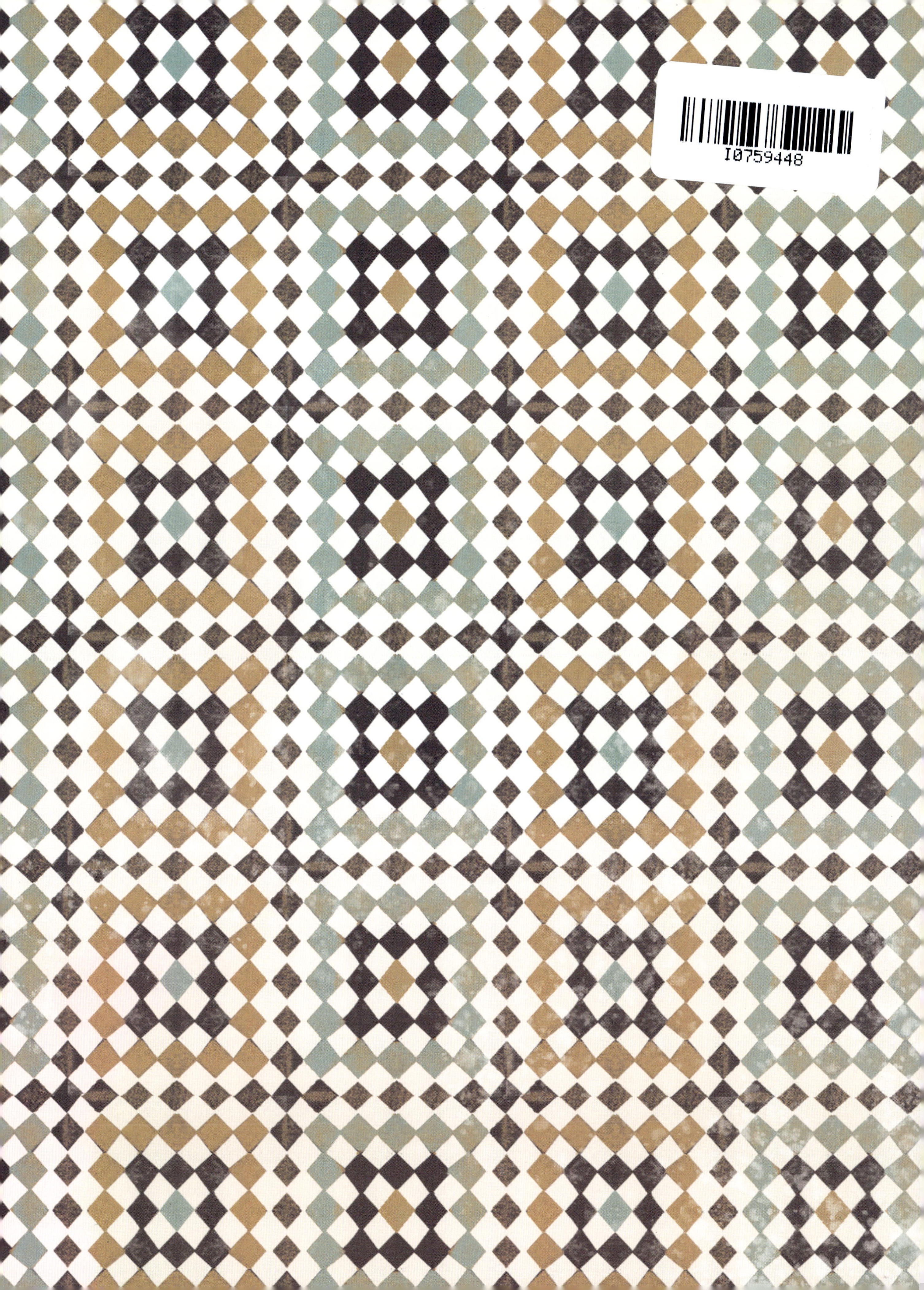
I0759448

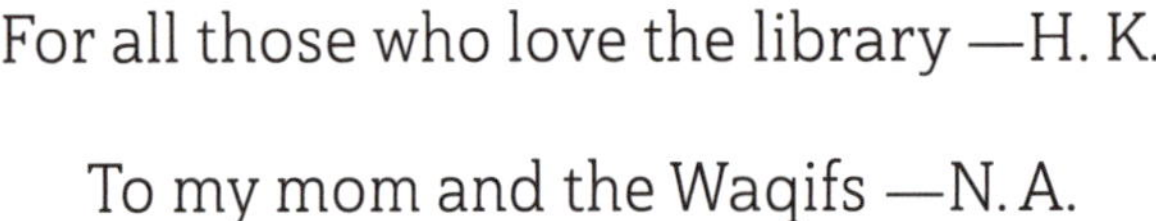

For all those who love the library —H. K.

To my mom and the Waqifs —N. A.

LEE & LOW BOOKS INC., 381 Park Avenue South, New York, NY 10016
leeandlow.com
Edited by Cheryl Klein
Book design by Ashley Halsey
Book production by The Kids at Our House
The text is set in Haboro Slab, with the display type in Basmala
The illustrations were created digitally
Manufactured in China by RR Donnelley
3 5 7 9 10 8 6 4 2
First Edition

FSC www.fsc.org MIX Paper | Supporting responsible forestry FSC® C144853

Library of Congress Cataloging-in-Publication Data
Names: Khan, Hena, author. | Adani, Nabila, 1991– illustrator.
Title: Behind my doors : the story of the world's oldest library / by Hena Khan; illustrated by Nabila Adani.
Description: First edition. | New York : Lee & Low Books, [2024] | Includes bibliographical references. | Audience: Ages 5–10. | Summary: Al-Qarawiyyin Library shares the true story of how it was originally founded by a Muslim woman in 859 in Fez, Morocco, and remains the oldest operating library in existence.
Identifiers: LCCN 2023009882 | ISBN 9781643794235 (hardcover) | ISBN 9781643797076 (ebk)
Subjects: LCSH: Khizānat al-Qarawīyīn—History—Juvenile literature. | Libraries—Morocco—History—Juvenile literature. | Al-Fihri, Fatima, approximately 800–880—Juvenile literature. | LCGFT: Picture books.
Classification: LCC Z858.K46 K47 2024 | DDC 027.064—dc23/eng/20230531
LC record available at https://lccn.loc.gov/2023009882

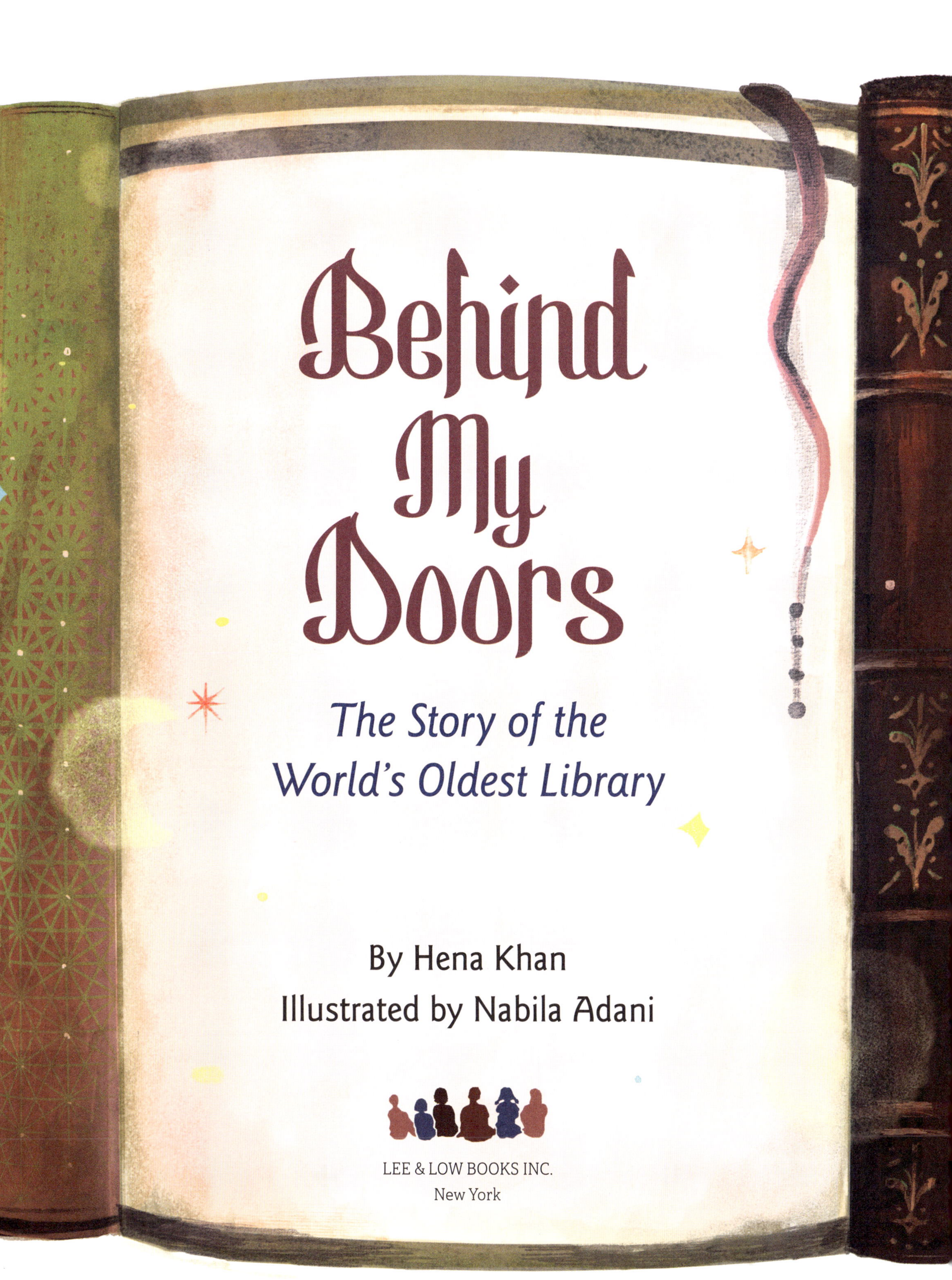

Behind My Doors

The Story of the World's Oldest Library

By Hena Khan
Illustrated by Nabila Adani

LEE & LOW BOOKS INC.
New York

Merhaba! I am Al-Qarawiyyin Library—the oldest library in the world. I've collected books in Fez, Morocco, for more than a thousand years. But the story I'm about to share is my very own.

I was born long, long ago, in the year 859, when a young woman named Fatima had a bold idea: to build a mosque and school for her community. I began as a small corner for books where Fatima spent hours reading, thinking, and dreaming . . .

... but I gradually grew into a grand building. My entrance faced a plaza connecting the narrow streets of the medina. Outside, coppersmiths banged on tools and merchants argued over prices all day.

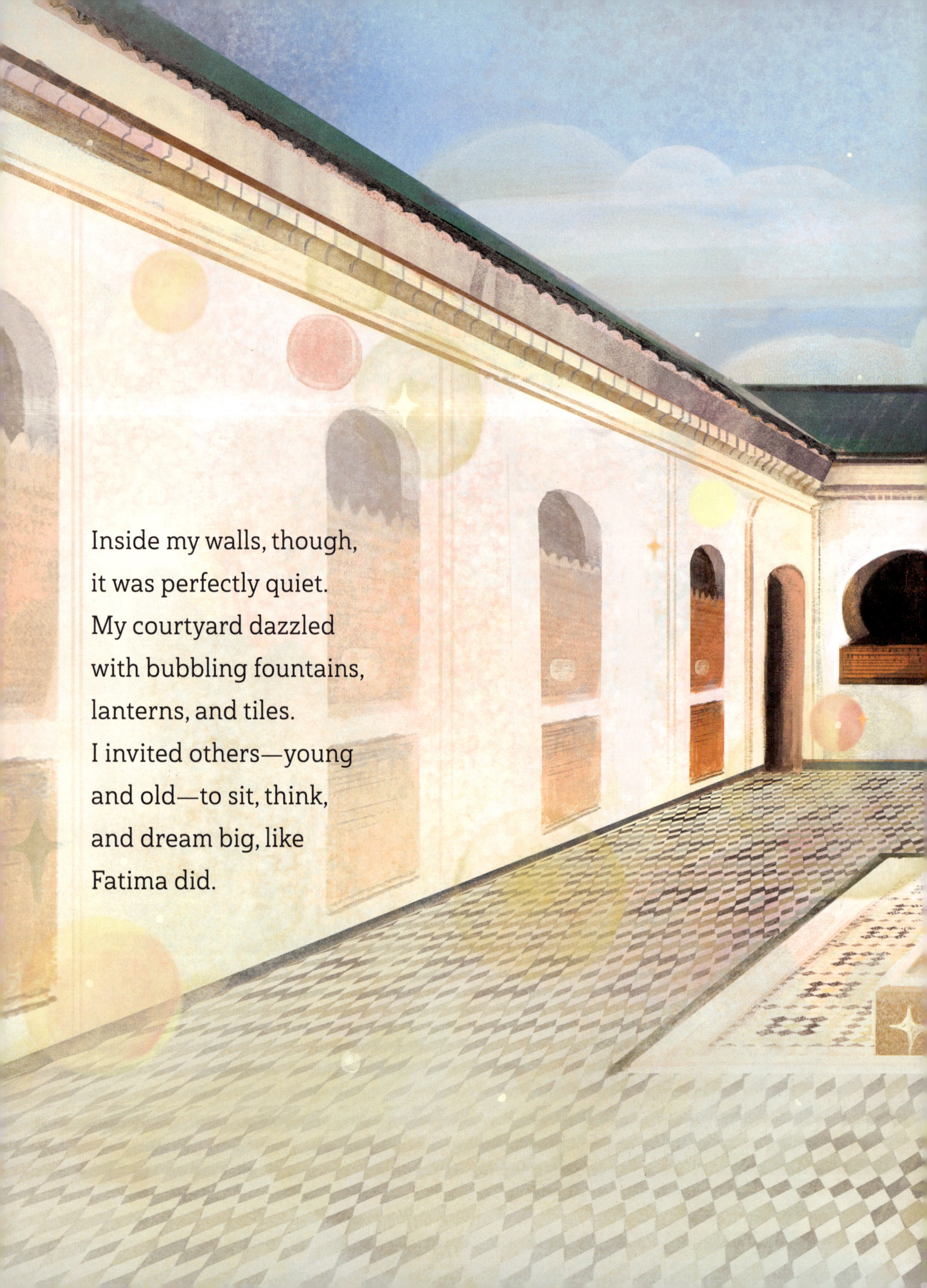

Inside my walls, though,
it was perfectly quiet.
My courtyard dazzled
with bubbling fountains,
lanterns, and tiles.
I invited others—young
and old—to sit, think,
and dream big, like
Fatima did.

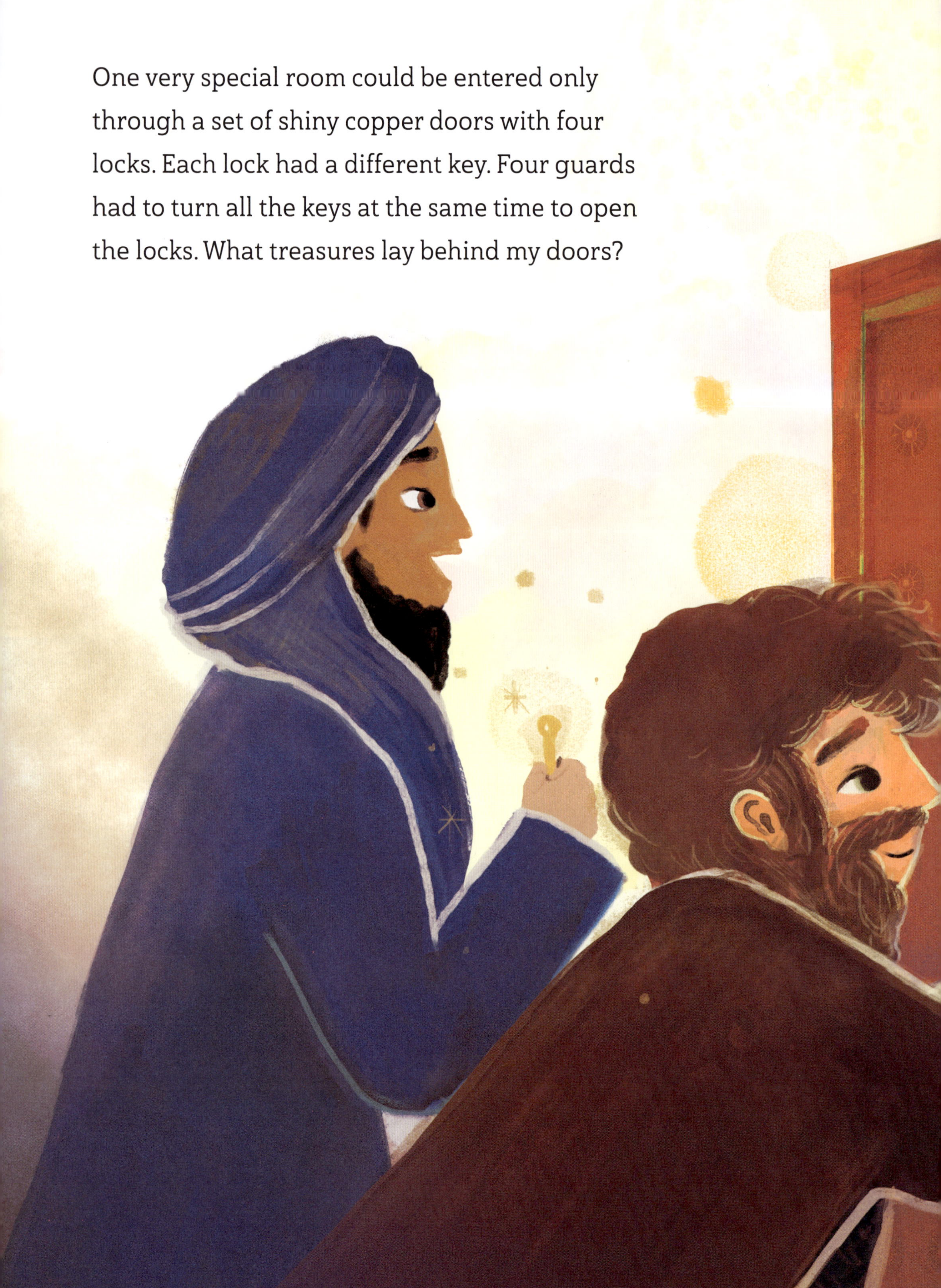

One very special room could be entered only through a set of shiny copper doors with four locks. Each lock had a different key. Four guards had to turn all the keys at the same time to open the locks. What treasures lay behind my doors?

Books—more precious than any jewels! In this room, I protected an ancient Quran written on camel-leather pages, a philosopher's drawings of the stars, and handwritten sheets with ink made from real gold.

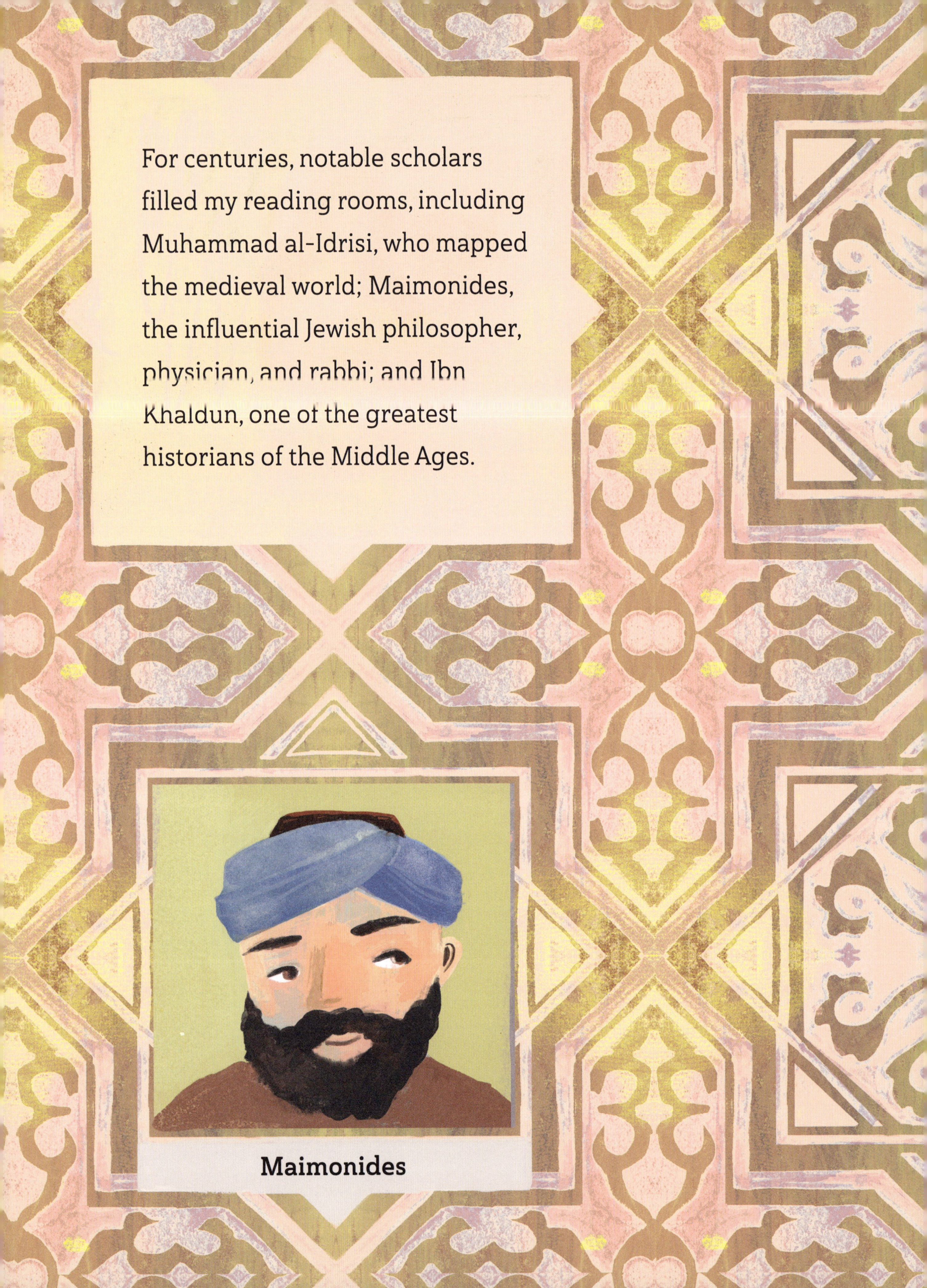

For centuries, notable scholars filled my reading rooms, including Muhammad al-Idrisi, who mapped the medieval world; Maimonides, the influential Jewish philosopher, physician, and rabbi; and Ibn Khaldun, one of the greatest historians of the Middle Ages.

Maimonides

Muhammad al-Idrisi

Ibn Khaldun

I listened while they and countless others discussed, debated, and made discoveries about science, math, medicine, and more. When they left, they took away knowledge to share with the world. But I kept the books safe with me.

Over time, kingdoms rose and fell around me. Once, I was almost destroyed by a terrible fire. Through it all, I stood tall, proud to serve the seekers of wisdom and searchers of truth.

Then, after many years passed,
fewer and fewer students began
to come through my doors.
I listened for the sound of
footsteps entering my courtyard.
But mostly I heard the clanging
of coppersmiths outside.

One day, a girl named Aziza passed by. With a book in her hand, she reminded me of someone from long ago—Fatima! As Aziza paused, I thought about her great-grandfather, who had traveled by donkey from his village faraway to visit me. I hoped she would enter, but Aziza gazed at my doors and kept walking.

I longed for my rooms to buzz with the spirit of learning again. But more and more chairs sat empty. My walls sagged with loneliness. My ceiling cracked. And when a branch of the Fez River began to flow beneath my floors, they grew damp, as if soaked with fallen tears. Without readers to appreciate my books, would they turn to dust, forgotten?

It took all my energy to stay upright. Just as I started to give up hope, a familiar face walked through my doors. It was the little girl from long before—Aziza! All grown up and now an award-winning architect, she had returned to Fez to help me.

Aziza and her team repaired my ceilings, walls, and tiles.

With their hard work, my floors were dry again, I glowed with brighter lights, and my doors gleamed like new.

Best of all, my books were saved, for anyone to read, forever.

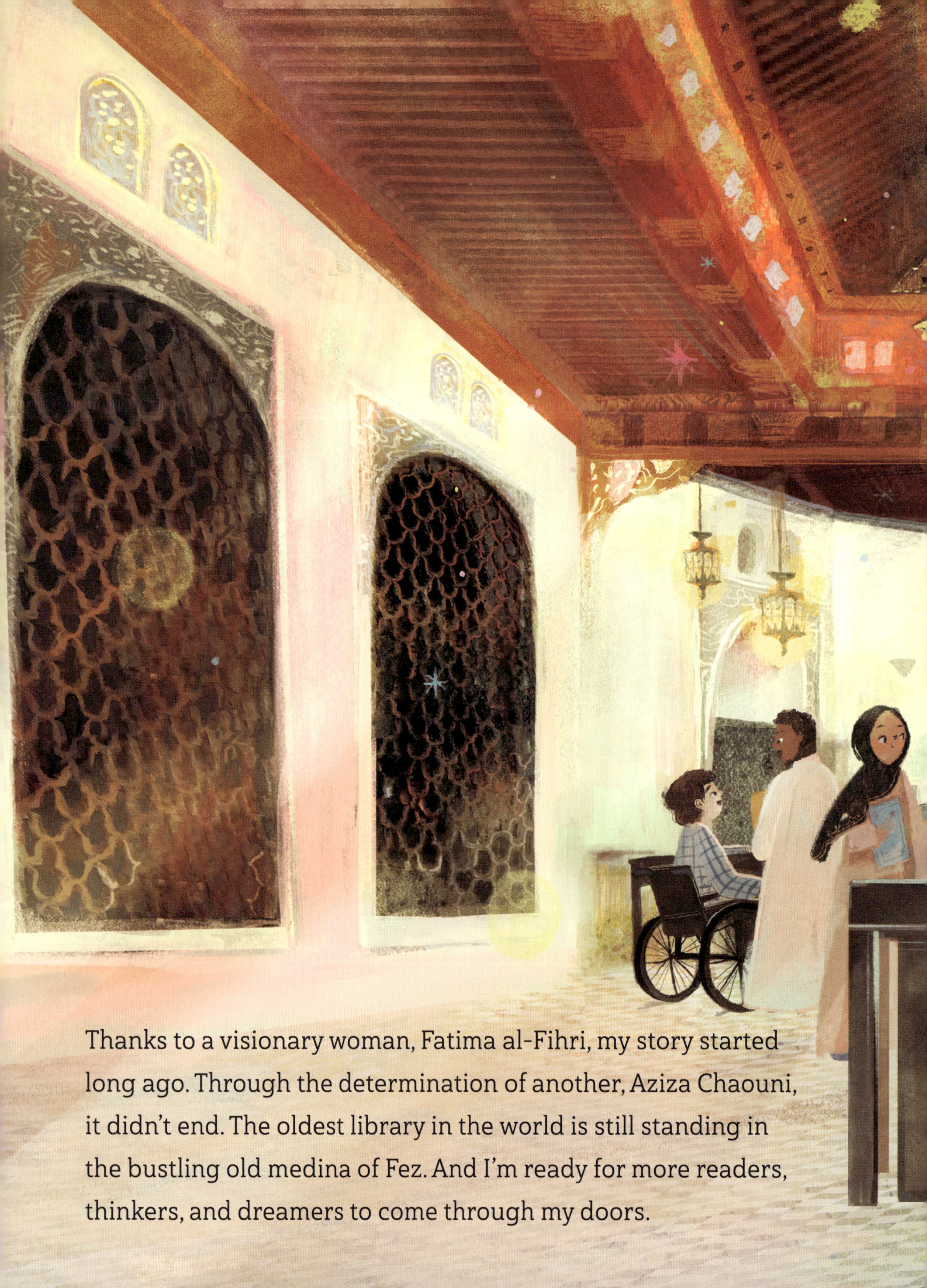

Thanks to a visionary woman, Fatima al-Fihri, my story started long ago. Through the determination of another, Aziza Chaouni, it didn't end. The oldest library in the world is still standing in the bustling old medina of Fez. And I'm ready for more readers, thinkers, and dreamers to come through my doors.

Author's Note

There's an old saying in Fez, Morocco, that people without books are like coppersmiths without tools. In 2019, I stood in a busy plaza in the old medina of Fez, in front of the doors of the Al-Qarawiyyin (pronounced "awl kar-ah-WEE-in") Library. I stared in awe at the building I had been researching and hoping to visit for years. As someone who grew up in my local library, I wanted to share the magic and wonder of this special place, which was founded by a Muslim woman.

In 859, Fatima al-Fihri, the daughter of a wealthy merchant, used her inheritance to build Al-Qarawiyyin Mosque; a school that eventually grew to become Al-Qarawiyyin University, the first degree-granting university in the world; and a library that served both institutions. Al-Qarawiyyin Library is now known as the oldest continuously operating library in existence.

Author Hena Khan in front of the Al-Qarawiyyan Library doors in Fez, Morocco.

Some of the important transfer of knowledge between North Africa and Europe throughout the Middle Ages is attributed to the library, which remained a significant center of learning for hundreds of years. However, after part of the university moved outside Fez in the 1960s, the library building was used less and needed serious repairs.

Aziza Chaouni, an architect who grew up in Fez, remembers passing by the library doors as a child. In 2012, she was hired by the government of Morocco to restore the building. Dr. Chaouni led the effort to reinforce the walls, add lighting, build a canal to divert water under the building, and help digitize the books. She shared with this book's creators that since there weren't existing blueprints for the library, the construction site was a mystery. Her team found that the library started inside the mosque and grew into two buildings, then three buildings. They discovered different layers as she figured out how to preserve it.

Dr. Chaouni's own great-grandfather traveled for days by donkey from his village to Al-Qarawiyyin University, where he spent countless hours in the library. In our conversation, she shared that her work felt like a tribute to him. The library reopened in 2017, and Dr. Chaouni is proud to preserve a part of her heritage and the legacy of Fatima al-Fihri. She hopes that the history of this special place will be widely known, and that the library will be accessible to all—for the next thousand years and beyond.

Glossary

Medina (meh-DEEN-ah): the word means "city" or "town" in modern Arabic, but it is also used to refer to the oldest part of a city in North Africa, which usually includes narrow streets, lots of historic sites, and markets.

Merhaba (MER-ha-ba): a casual greeting in Arabic, such as "hello."

Quran (kor-ahn): the Muslim holy book.

References

Bennett, Charlie, Ameet Doshi, Wendy Hagenmaier, and Fred Rascoe (hosts). "Reimagining the Oldest Library in the World." *Lost in the Stacks* on *WREK Radio,* Episode 308 (June 24, 2016). http://hdl.handle.net/1853/55377

Lewis, Danny. "The World's Oldest Working Library Will Soon Open Its Doors to the Public." *Smithsonian Magazine*, July 13, 2016. www.smithsonianmag.com/smart-news/worlds-oldest-working-library-will-soon-open-to-the-public-180959670/.

Marozzi, Justin. *Islamic Empires: Fifteen Cities That Define a Civilization*. Penguin UK, August 29, 2019.